THE
Archive Photographs
SERIES

WILLINGTON

The underground stables at Brancepeth Colliery. The horses were able to rest here after their shift was finished. Several horsekeepers were employed to see to their well being and it was usual for one person to be responsible for up to fifteen animals.

THE
Archive Photographs
SERIES

WILLINGTON

Compiled by
Olive Linge

CHALFORD

First published 1997
Copyright © Olive Linge, 1997

The Chalford Publishing Company
St Mary's Mill, Chalford,
Stroud, Gloucestershire, GL6 8NX

ISBN 0 7524 1073 3

Typesetting and origination by
The Chalford Publishing Company
Printed in Great Britain by
Bailey Print, Dursley, Gloucestershire

Ponies at Brancepeth A Pit, 1929. Although conditions were hardly ideal for these animals, they were usually treated with kindness and well thought of by their handlers.

Contents

A pedestrian walkway which spanned the railway line. This picture was taken just before demolition, which began on 4 September 1971, and shows the High Street with, in the immediate foreground on the right, what used to be the Railway Station Hotel.

Introduction

I do hope that the readers of this book will enjoy looking back over the years with fond memories of people and places long gone.

Maybe, as they turn the pages, they will see a familiar face of a relative, friend, or in some cases probably themselves. It is not meant to be a lesson in history, but just a nostalgic reminder of how Willington and its people once were.

The village lies by the River Wear with Bishop Auckland four miles to the south, and the majestic City of Durham seven miles to the north east.

Although there were no early settlements here, the Roman road which joined up the forts of Binchester and Lanchester can still be traced.

The name itself dates back to Saxon times but it wasn't until a Norman Lord built his manor house at nearby Brancepeth that we see any significant development with the building of cottages to house his estate workers.

By 1839 records show that there were shops, a smithy, inns, and even a private school, catering for a population of around 230. This figure soon increased with the mining of coal which began in 1840 and from then on Willington, like Topsy from *Uncle Tom's Cabin*, 'just growed', reaching its peak in the 1920s.

The names synonymous with the pits were those of Straker and Love, two wealthy mine owners. Not always well thought of by their employees, especially during the many strikes, they nevertheless brought good fortune to the village.

As is common with every other pit community, it has seen its fair share of prosperity, poverty and tragedy, and over the last 150 years some dramatic changes.

The closure of the pits and the railway in the 1960s could have sounded the death knell for the village but Willington has survived with its dignity intact.

Brancepeth Colliery in its heyday. In the foreground, on the left, the stables, to the right, Gas Cottages and the Victoria Club.

One
Places

A warning sign erected by the AA on the approach to the village.

St Stephen's church, 1916. Built in 1857, within the then parish of Brancepeth, the first stained glass window was dedicated to the memory of Major General Mills. Some of the earliest parish magazines show some interesting facts. One in particular, for Easter 1891, records some of the outgoings; amongst these being water – 12s 3d, and wine – £1 0s 9d. Obviously not Cana in Galilee.

Jubilee Bridge, 1907. Built to commemorate the Jubilee of Queen Victoria, this bridge crossed the River Wear between Willington and Newfield. It was demolished a number of years ago and replaced with a much wider bridge more able to cope with the increased amount of traffic. At the time of her Diamond Jubilee, the park to the right was given to the village by Lord Boyne and sixty poplar trees planted to mark the occasion.

Low Willington, 1904. A time when traffic was virtually none existent and life was lived at a much more leisurely pace. This was the site of the old toll bar, and I am told that a stream used to cross the road here. There is a lovely old wicker pram on the left.

A summer deluge causing problems for this bus at Low Willington. During the strike of 1921 the public house, on the right, frequently provided a midday meal for up to one hundred and fifty children.

Park Villas. These were flats situated opposite the war memorial which have now been replaced by a small housing estate known as Kingsmead.

Low Willington, 1909. The house on the right, with the sign on the upper part of the wall, was once the Bluebell public house, much altered over the years and is now converted to housing.

The Co-operative Store, *c.* 1930. Opened in the 1870s in Commercial Street – where it was possible to buy anything from an 'Armchair to a Zinc bath tub' – this store paid a dividend on all goods purchased, which could be drawn half annually, or left in the account to gain interest. An early recorded 'divi' was nearly four shillings in the pound, but of course at that time £1 could have probably bought a week's groceries. St Stephen's Close now stands on this site.

A Co-op advertisement, taken from a chapel magazine, 1924.

The Bridge, *c.* 1970. A picture taken from Commercial Street looking towards High Street, with a clear view of the bridge built to span the railway line. To the right are: Thomas the fruiterer, F. Walton the butcher and Angelo Rea's ice cream shop, now a cafe.

The Bridge, *c.* 1970. The same bridge as the previous picture, this time looking towards Commercial Street. On the right is Moores stores, now the chemists. The small building next to it had many occupants over the years but will probably be best remembered by older people as the cobblers' shop belonging to Mr Horner. The library and a newly built nursery now occupy the waste land seen just beyond.

14

Station Cottages. These were built just behind the railway station to house railway workers. The library now occupies this site.

The railway station, *c.* 1969. It looks like a long wait for this little boy, Nigel Linge, as the last train left some time ago, but he hasn't given up and can still be seen on station platforms in Lancashire waiting for steam trains.

The Durham platform with Mr Brown, Mr Watson and Mr Wilson, three of the station staff. Dating back to the 1850s, this was the main line between Bishop Auckland and Durham and was much used to transport coal and coke. It is recorded that on 23 October 1869 twelve runaway wagons from Brancepeth Colliery came hurtling through this station running head on into a passenger train unloading people at Hunwick. The engine driver and fireman were both killed and several passengers hurt.

Chapel Street. The wrought iron archway on the left was the entrance to the United Methodist chapel which was demolished together with these houses to make way for a health centre and car park. The surgery now stands on the site of the garages on the right.

Short's Shop. The shop stood next to the Council School and was much used by local children on their way to school. When these premises closed their entire stock of sweets was distributed to the children who had given them so much trade.

The Council School, 1910. The school was opened on 8 January 1892 in Chapel Street and originally consisted of nine classrooms to accommodate children up to fourteen years of age. Today, pupils only stay here until they are eleven, when they transfer to the Comprehensive School in Hall Lane. The first pupil recorded was Richard G. Render who, fifty years later, became School Chairman. The first Headmaster was Mr Taylor.

Cold Storage. These buildings were built during the Second World War to house emergency supplies of food. The buildings were a common sight on any train journey; all built to a seemingly identical design and standing adjacent to the railway line. A nursing home now occupies this site.

The ice cream man, Albert Rea, on his rounds on Dene Estate. He is pictured in Appleton Crescent.

Luxmoore Avenue. This street was part of the first council estate to be built in Willington during the 1920s, all the houses having flush toilets, bathrooms and gardens. This must have seemed like sheer luxury in those days. The lady standing outside number twenty-six is Mrs Dawson.

Gardner Avenue. This is the same estate as the previous picture. The house with the cross is the home of Robert and Mary Failes and their six children.

The Brancepeth Hotel public house. Now the site of St Thomas' Close, this was the Brancepeth Hotel, situated at the bottom of the colliery road.

Cross Street. This was a row of ten houses built practically within the colliery yard and I understand that this is where the ambulance station was later erected.

The Bridge End, 1926. Now the site of the Zebra Crossing, this was a popular meeting place for men going to and from work at the colliery. In the foreground on the right, was Pilkington's, now a dress shop and Graham's now a fish shop. The Mitre public house and the other properties seen on the same side of the street were demolished. Metcalfe's, on the left, in later years was quite substantially reduced in size and became Moores stores referred to on p. 14.

The High Street. A view taken from much the same position as the previous picture but this time showing the opposite side of High Street.

The Empress Cinema just prior to demolition, having become a Bingo Hall in later years. In its heyday the Empress was a popular place of entertainment and had a change of programme three times a week.

The demise of the Empress. The ornate stage was the last part to succumb to the demolition crew.

Middleton's. One of the oldest shops in the High Street, built prior to 1900 and demolished together with most of the other properties which backed on to the colliery rows. It is now an open space with grassed areas and flower beds.

WHICH IS THE BEST HOUSE IN THE DISTRICT
For First=Class Goods in Groceries, Provisions, &c.

WHY JOHN MIDDLETON,

HIGH STREET, WILLINGTON.

Famous for the Finest Ceylon Tea procurable, and the Cheapest House for
Flour, Butter, Lard, Ham, Bacon, Jams, &c.

An advertisement taken from the Wesleyan chapel magazine, 1899.

Paxton's. Jennie, Ernest and Mrs Paxton outside their printers and stationers shop at the top end of High Street. It is now a hardware store but, to older people, this part of the street is still referred to as 'Paxton's Corner'.

E. PAXTON,

The Printer of this Handbook, for

PRINTING, BOOKBINDING,

and STATIONERY.

Prompt Personal Attention to all Orders.
Note the Address—

88, High St., Willington

An advertisement from the Willington Wesleyan chapel magazine of 1924.

The shop in the High Street belonging to Mr Coates, a printer, who was responsible for creating quite a record of photographic history of the village during the first half of this century. Some of his work is featured in this book. This display is for the Coronation of George VI and Queen Elizabeth.

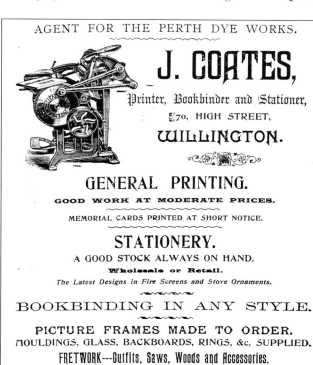

AGENT FOR THE PERTH DYE WORKS.

J. COATES,

Printer, Bookbinder and Stationer,

70, HIGH STREET,

WILLINGTON.

GENERAL PRINTING.

GOOD WORK AT MODERATE PRICES.

MEMORIAL CARDS PRINTED AT SHORT NOTICE.

STATIONERY.

A GOOD STOCK ALWAYS ON HAND.

Wholesale or Retail.

The Latest Designs in Fire Screens and Stove Ornaments.

BOOKBINDING IN ANY STYLE.

PICTURE FRAMES MADE TO ORDER.

MOULDINGS, GLASS, BACKBOARDS, RINGS, &c. SUPPLIED.

FRETWORK---Outfits, Saws, Woods and Accessories.

AGENT FOR THE ROYAL FIRE INSURANCE COMPANY.

An advertisement taken from a magazine of 1899 referring to his previous shop lower down the High Street.

The Tea Room of the Parish Hall all set out for its first visitors at the opening of the new hall, the previous one being on the site of the Empress. No paper tablecloths in those days but beautiful laced edged ones all probably hand crafted by the church ladies. When the church could find no further use for this building it was sold and converted into an hotel.

The paddling pool and bandstand in the Dene. Remains of the bandstand can still be seen today but the pool is now overgrown. During the last few years children from the Catholic School, together with The Groundwork Trust, have erected hand carved benches depicting woodland scenes throughout this wood.

The High Street. The first shop on the left belonged to Cottrells for a great number of years, and the one with the sun blind was a grocers. The Royal Tent came next, but it, together with all the other properties situated on the same side of the street as far as the second telegraph pole, are all long gone. The single storey building, seen next to the Royal Tent, belonged to the Salvation Army and was home to the Red Shield Club referred to on p. 72. On the right is Simpson's Garage.

An advertisement from 1924 for Simpson's Garage in Hutton Terrace. The business later moved to premises in High Street.

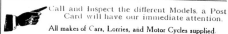

The top end of High Street looking towards Durham showing, on the right, Armoury, a gentleman's outfitter, Fryer's shoe shop and, on the left, the milk cart belonging to Herbert Bond.

The West End. There must be some special reason to warrant a Police Sergeant to be on duty at Hunwick Lane End.

Hunwick Lane End in the early 1920s. Behind the trees on the left stands Laurel House, once the home of the Rutter family, who ran a small factory manufacturing baking powder etc. It was in this garden that a Roman milestone was discovered on Sunday 1 June 1941 by John J. Wilkinson.

An advertisement from 1912 showing the products of the factory named in the previous picture.

Hunwich Lane, Willington.

The following set of pictures show the demise of the pit heap. A distant view of the pit heap showing just how much it dominated the sky line, taken when it was still in use.

The first stage. Taken from approximately the same position as the last picture, showing the heap in the first stage of its removal, with the tracks now dismantled.

The second stage. The peaks are now completely removed and in the process of being flattened. On the right is the Miners' Welfare Hall and on the left, Burnington Drive.

The final stage. All gone! Demolition is now completed and the area landscaped.

The Miners' Welfare Hall, c. 1930. It was opened around 1927 and designed especially to provide leisure facilities for colliery workers. Here they could follow many pursuits, the billiard room and bowling green being the two most popular. Mr Brumwell, the gentleman standing on the left, was responsible for the upkeep of the grounds and at one time had quite a display of topiary. A canopy was later built over the arched windows to provide shelter for spectators. It has been much altered in recent years having been given to the local Council.

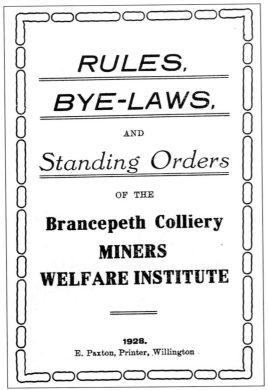

RULES,

BYE-LAWS,

AND

Standing Orders

OF THE

Brancepeth Colliery

MINERS

WELFARE INSTITUTE

1928.

E. Paxton, Printer, Willington.

A Rule Book from 1927. One of the rules states that, 'Should any member swear, talk profanely or obscenely, or enter the Institute in a state of intoxication he shall be immediately expelled and dealt with by the Committee'.

St John's church, Sunnybrow. It was built in 1885 to serve as a parish church for Sunnybrow, Helmington Row and part of Willington. It was demolished in 1979.

The wedding of Donald Kenneth Linge and Olive Failes took place at St John's church on 27 December 1948. The best man was Sydney Aspinall and the bridesmaid was Joan Dawson. The service was conducted by the Revd Lacy-Jones. The photograph gives a whole new concept on the meaning of solemnization!

The bridge which spanned the railway line at Sunnybrow. On the left, is the Institute, on the right, Bridge Street and beyond that, the prefabs built to relieve the vast shortage of housing following the Second World War.

Looking in the opposite direction to the previous picture, towards the old part of Sunnybrow which, in the 1800s, could boast a brewery.

The West End. It has hardly changed, apart from the design of the bus and the lack of traffic.

Watling Terrace, 1928. As the name suggests these houses were built parallel to the Roman Road.

Boggle Hole Bank. It was a much steeper bank in those days, having to cross over the Bowden Close railway line at Cummings Bridge. The boys seem to be enjoying the snow, not something they could do with present day traffic. There appears to be one lone rider, and a pony and trap towards the top of the bank. With the arrival of public transport it was a common occurrence for buses to get stuck here. Too bad if you worked in Crook; it was then 'shanks' pony'. I know, I did it several times!

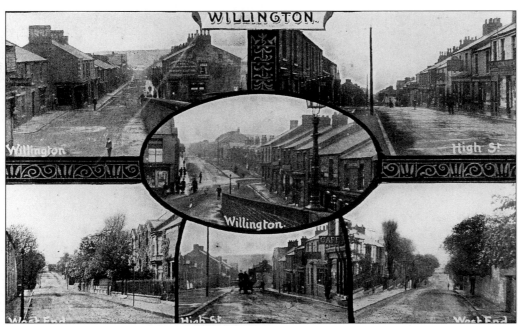

Six views of Willington taken in the early 1920s.

A Bird's Eye View. A view taken from the pit heap showing Hall Lane Estate still under construction, the railway station still working and the police station still standing. In the foreground, on the left, can be seen part of Single Russell Place, now replaced by Bourne Way.

A view from the pit heap. In the foreground are some of the colliery rows; on the left is Albert Street next to Catherine, Tyne, Wear and York Streets. The tall building with the eight windows, to the left of the middle, was the United Methodist chapel

and beyond that the Cold Storage. In the distance, on the left, is the old part of Sunnybrow and Hunwick Brick Works. To the right, in the background, are the prefabs, and middle right, Dene Estate.

A good view of the Catholic church and Cumberland Terrace, sometimes referred to as Taffy Lane. In the background, to the left, can be seen the Burn Farm.

Two
People

The Meadow Dairy girls, *c.* 1946. Left to right, Olive Failes, Agnes Vizard and Audrey Slack. A very popular shop with a good reputation, as the name suggests, for dairy produce. These windows had to be washed every day and the display emptied every Saturday night ready for the new one on a Monday morning. White starched cap and overalls had to be scrupulously clean. The building is now living accommodation.

A group of church members taken in the vicarage garden. I think that the array of hats would not go amiss at Ascot, although I doubt very much whether any of these ladies would participate in gambling!

Members of the St Stephen's Mothers' Union at the Parish Hall with the pit heap in the background. The society was founded by Mary Summer and incorporated by Royal Charter in 1926. Its main objective was to 'uphold the sanctity of marriage and defend the home from the dangers of intemperance, betting, gambling, bad language and other evils'.

Chapel Street Young Men's Bible Class, 1936. This chapel, formerly known as The New Connexion, was erected in 1855 at a cost of £1,200. It was described as a fine substantial stone building with a circular gallery. The site was donated by Lord Boyne but its main benefactor was Joseph Love, part owner of the local collieries. The health centre now stands on the site of the chapel.

The Primitive Methodist Concert Party in the early 1900s. Information gleaned from the back of a postcard sent in 1905 mentions just how successful this group was, also the fact that they had formed a cycling club.

The Wesleyan Christian Brotherhood Sunday School outing on 22 July 1906. It was an annual event, much looked forward to by the children, and probably the one day in the year when they would leave the village. Here they are assembled in Lydia Street, ready to march the few yards to the station where they would board the train for maybe Roker or Shields.

Sunday School Children from one of the local chapels. Obviously there had been some kind of collection. They are very up market dolls, one of them in the centre appears to be wearing a cap and gown! The photograph was probably taken in the 1920s judging by the little one's hat!

Members of the Wesleyan Sunday School.

The Wesleyan Ladies Concert Party dates back to the late 1800s, but not these ladies of course! In the official handbook of 1899 a 'Winter's Concert' is advertised with seat prices of between 3d and 1/-.

The Church Lads' Brigade, *c.* 1920. The Church Lads' Brigade was first formed in Fulham on 21 July 1891 by Captain Walter Gee, starting with a membership of approximately thirty to forty boys and increasing to over one million in 1924. During the First World War twenty-two Victoria Crosses were awarded to members of this society. This picture shows the local branch formed in 1894.

Members of the Catholic church with Father Holmes, seated second from the left in the second row.

The First Aid Troupe of the Boy Scouts who had obviously been demonstrating their skills on the 'victim' on the stretcher.

The Memorial, 1908. A memorial in St Stephen's cemetery was erected in memory of Thomas Barton, who risked his life to rescue a child from a burning building in Railway Terrace. Six weeks later he was killed in the pit, by a fall of stone. Public subscription provided this tribute to a local hero.

A Celebration, *c.* 1900. This is one of the oldest pictures in the collection. I believe that this was part of the celebration of the Relief of Mafeking, during the reign of Queen Victoria. The public house on the right was the Court Inn, later to be renamed The Mitre, now demolished. The cottages were some of the first colliery houses and the notice board on the gable end was used to display which pit would be working that day.

Wear Street, 1928. Taken in the days when there was a real community spirit and people took a pride in their surroundings. Although compared to today's standards, living conditions were quite poor, however, one could walk down any colliery row and see steps scrubbed and whitened with scouring stone. For some reason most houses seemed to have a display of egg cups in their small pantry windows. Wear Street was just behind the High Street and is now a grassed area with flower beds.

Three families living in Mill Street all sharing one yard and one earth closet. They are Mr and Mrs Atkinson, Mr and Mrs Suffield and Mr and Mrs Pearsall and their families.

The Pearsall Family; Amy, Lily, Richard and baby Arthur.

Drinkers in the old band room yard looking towards Railway Terrace. They are probably customers from the Brancepeth Hotel. For some reason one of the men appears to be nursing a doll. St Thomas' Close now stands on this site.

Labour Camp, 1937. Unemployed men from Willington leaving Bishop Auckland to work mainly in the sugar beet fields and forests in Brandon, Norfolk. Prior to the Second World War the long term unemployed were sent to Labour Camps and if they refused they lost their benefits. Conditions in these camps were usually very poor and after paying for their weekly board and lodgings they were left with less than four shillings. Included are: B. Dunleavy, T. Melvin and Mr Lee.

Winners of the Leek Show, taken, I believe, at the Victoria Club. Much rivalry exists between the competitors and it has been known for men to sit up all night guarding their precious trenches. Great secrecy abounds between the men concerning weird concoctions they have for feeding these vegetables. If some of these tales are true, I'm sure that they will be deemed unsuitable for human consumption!

A local branch of the Grand Order of Buffaloes, c. 1920.

Prize Band, 1931. The Silver Prize Band was formed in 1880 and proved to be much in demand for special events. In the 1908 season they won fifteen prize titles spending in that year £350 on new instruments. Brancepeth Colliery was added to the title sometime after 1914.

A Band Concert held in the presence of Dr and Mrs Crichton (seated in the centre), a much respected local G.P. and his wife.

Some kind of parade, maybe on Gala Day, taken towards the top end of High Street, probably on their way to the Welfare Hall. Mr Ainsley, the bandmaster, can be seen on the left. It was a time when Willington had cobbled streets.

Members of the Miners' Variety Concert Party having just taken part in a broadcast for the BBC Radio in 1938. The gentleman, second from the left, middle row, is Jack Hetherington who can be seen with his talking dolls.

A gathering of the Wednesday Club, in the Primitive chapel school room, *c.* 1950. This was a weekly social get together where dancing was the main activity. Included are: Emily Aspinall, Mrs Blackett, Mrs Kidd, Mrs Scarr, Mrs Walker and the small child Joyce Walker.

The Willingtonians. It was a regular event for this particular jazz band to take part in the national finals, held annually in Great Yarmouth. This picture must have been taken in its early days as they don't appear to have many medals, whereas, in its later years these sashes would have been practically covered.

Three
Schools

Standard Six from Willington Council School, 1906.

Class Three from a local school but no clues as to which one. In the early part of the twentieth century one thinks of poverty but these children are exceptionally well dressed with beautiful lace collars and some in velvet suits.

Pupils from the Church of England School which was situated at Low Willington. It was built in 1851 on land donated by the Hamilton Russells of Brancepeth Castle.

Children in class at the Council Infants School in Chapel Street. Note the slates still in use.

Children of varying ages from the Catholic School. On the right is Father Aloysious Hosten, a Belgian priest who studied Theology at the English School in Bruges. Ordained in July 1869 by Bishop Chadwick, he commenced his duties in the village in 1877 and remained here until his death in 1923.

The Catholic School in the 1950s with Miss Pickering on the right. To mention a few names: M. Cunningham, A. and M. Dunleavy, A. Lamb and E. Traynor.

A class from the Council School, *c.* 1930. Mr Jennings, the Headmaster, is on the right.

Another group from the Council School.

The Council School, 1950. Mrs Sproates and her pupils posing with goalkeeper Jackie Snowdon and the F.A. Amateur Challenge Cup won in 1950 by Willington Football Team.

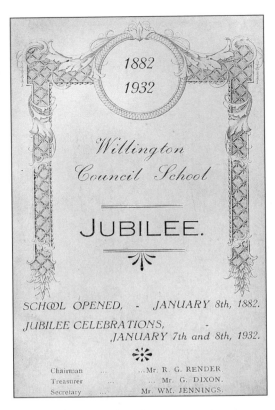

The Council School Jubilee, 1932. It celebrated fifty years of this school. The Supper Menu reads as follows: Stuffed Roast Pork, Boiled Tongue, Boiled Ham, and Pease Pudding and Pickles. To follow, Mince and Apple Tarts, Variety Cakes, Fruit Salad and Cream. Tea and Coffee.

Part of the celebrations which took place to mark the centenary of the Council School in 1982.

Four
Transport

The 'Store' butcher's cart at the bottom of the colliery road with Captain, the horse and its driver Mr Ronnie Coatsworth.

Mr Downs, a tinsmith, who used to tour the area selling his wares. I understand that this picture was taken outside a house in Sunnybrow, which would appear to need more than his skills!

Richardson's milk cart taken, I think, at the bottom of Snowdon Terrace. In those days milk would be delivered to the door in churns where the householder would provide a jug and milk would be measured out in gills.

The ice cream man pictured, I am told, in Park View or as it is often referred to by older people, Klondike.

The 'Store' greengrocer outside Single Russell Place, with Albert Street just in front of the pit heap. These two streets were demolished and Bourne Way built on the site of Single Russell Place.

A fleet of Bond's buses outside their depot in Prospect Terrace. It's a family firm which started life in the first part of the century and who are still in business at the present time. There is an excellent view of the pit heap with the tub about to reach the top where it would automatically tip its waste from the pits.

A Bond's bus waiting outside the local branch of Crook Co-op. The Empress is behind the bus. The shop with the 'Woodbine' advertisement is that of Lily Holmes, a ladies' milliner and haberdasher

Blarney Bar. Advertising tobacco would not be considered politically correct today. The poster displaying the anniversary notice is outside the Pentecostal church in the West End of Willington.

A service bus struggling to get through to Durham after a summer deluge at Low Willington.

Two charabancs leave the Brancepeth Hotel to take the lads off on a day's outing in 1911. In the background, on the left, can be seen the coal drop at the bottom of the colliery road.

Willington Empire Jaunt, 1912. Yet another outing, this time the ladies have been allowed to join the menfolk. It seems like quite a precarious way to travel especially when taking corners!

Leaving for Bishop Auckland is one of the last trains to use this line. Railway workers' houses can be seen on the left and the Empire Picture House in the background, on the right.

Empty trucks waiting in the sidings between Sunnybrow and Willington in the early 1960s. Kathleen and Elizabeth Dewey are the two children.

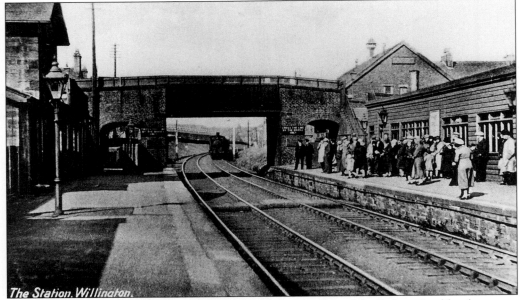

The Station, Willington.

In the days of steam, a train arriving to pick up passengers bound for Bishop Auckland.

This biplane landed on the outskirts of the village, some say towards Brancepeth and others Sunnybrow, in 1911. It belonged to an American aviator by the name of Cody; no, not Buffalo Bill but Samuel Franklin Cody, who was the first man to fly 1,390 feet over Britain in 1908.

68

Five

Wartime

The Fund Raisers, 1941. The Bolam Brothers did a great deal to raise funds during the Second World War. This particular War Weapons Week raised over £1,433. Various other events took place, amongst them being: Wings for Victory which raised £529, Salute the Soldier £1,414, Flower Class of Frigate (H.M.S. *Clarkia*) £741. I remember these two men touring the village with a huge block of wood, representing Hitler's coffin, and for one penny you could knock in a nail!

The Cenotaph, c. 1920. One of the many ceremonies taking place during the early 1920s to commemorate the lives of servicemen and women lost during the First World War. This one is inscribed with names from Willington, Page Bank and Oakenshaw.

The Peace Parade marching from Commercial Street to High Street in 1918. I am told that practically the whole village turned out to celebrate the end of the First World War.

St Stephen's church Lych Gate, *c*. 1950, which, I understand, had been erected in memory of the people of the parish who had lost their lives during the Second World War.

Dad's Army, *c*. 1940. The members of the Home Guard include: Messers Dover, Graham, Hetherington, Holmes, Paterson and Wearmouth.

Members of the British Legion who have been busy making poppy wreaths. Standing, left to right: Mrs Hodgson, Mr Wilson, Mrs Moore, Mrs Adamson, Mr Reynolds, Mrs Walton, Mrs Aston, Mrs Canvin and Mr and Mrs Small. Seated: Mesdames Dennis, Lines, Moore, Weir, Wilkinson and Ford.

The Canteen, c. 1940. Volunteers at the Red Shield Club set up the canteen in the Salvation Army building in High Street, during the Second World War. Here servicemen and women could drop in for a meal or, in some cases, a shoulder to cry on. Each morning a van would be loaded with sandwiches and a huge urn of tea, in order to visit soldiers practising on the firing range at nearby Oakenshaw. Standing, left to right: Captain Levene (Salvation Army), Emily Lines, Mrs Atkinson, Mesdames Lines, Sally Painter, Mrs Reynolds, Canvin, Richardson. Seated: Mrs Stobbart and Mrs Painter.

Celebrating victory in 1945 are a group of Dene Estate residents, in the school room of the United Methodist chapel.

Yet another victory celebration with residents from Luxmoore and Gardner Avenues. To name all but two: Mrs Parkin, Richardson, Bibby, Booth, Auton, Robinson, Aberdeen, Brown, Dent, Osborne, Armstrong, Hetherington and Dawson.

Victory, 1945. Enjoying victory celebrations well into the early hours, in the square on Gardner Avenue.

More victory celebrations in 1945. This is on the opposite side of the street to the previous picture, this time in the square on Appleton Crescent.

Six

Sport

A Ladies Football Team, 1921. Lots of people seem to think that women playing football is a modern phenomenon but this picture tells a different story. Names can be put to some of these ladies but maybe not in the correct order. To name some: Mesdames Bolam, Jackson, Collin, Martin, Moore, Blackett and the Misses Scratcher, Gatiss and Gatiss.

The cricket team of 1905 with Messers: Mundell, Holmes, Gibbon, Powley, Holmes, Bell, Stephenson, Newton, Heslop, Foster, Arrowsmith, Wynn, Allison, Wilson and seated in the striped blazer, Captain Howe (Colliery Manager).

Willington cricket team of 1938 showing the colliery in the background.

The cricket team of 1944 in the Colliery Manager's garden. Included are: T. Slack, J. Coe, A. Davison, F. Dover, B. Bulman and A. Morton.

Yet another team, showing on the left, the umpire Mr F. Sowerby.

T. HUNTLEY   B. SCHOFIELD
J. GIBSON   W. GIBSON   J. PEARS   S. SMALL   J. COUGHLIN   T. TEASDALE   T. FOX   J. ANDERSON   T. SMALL   R. WOOD (Vice-Pres.)
J. BOYD (Hon. Sec)   W. J. BUTLER, Esq. J.P.   T. GEDDES   R. PHILLIPSON (Capt.)   W. PROUD   W. MITCHELL (Vice-Capt.)   R. PEARS   J. H. ARMOURY (President.)   H. FARROW (Treasurer.)   J. CLEMENT
J. GIBSON   W. HOLMES   E. PHILLIPSON   R. CARLING   J. E. SERSTON   T. DAND   A. BELL.

Bishop Auckland.

The Temperance Football Club of 1909, winners of the Auckland District League, Boothroyd Cup and Crook and District Nursing Cup.

Willington A.F.C., 1925-26.

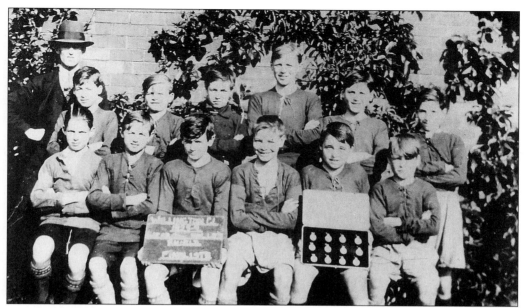

The Council School team of 1928 with their teacher Mr O. Holmes. Back row: N. Magee, J. Newell, J. Henfry, H. Wood, E. Hudson, D. Robinson. Front row: L. Clement, J. Richardson, H. Spence, I. Stephenson, E. Bell, H. Kemp.

The League of Youth, 1929.

The Wesleyan football team of the 1930s who played on a field at Sunnybrow and had quite a good track record. Back row, fourth from the left, is Tommy Melvin, standing next to the goalkeeper, Thomas Failes.

Kensington Villa, 1932. This team were all residents of either Albert, Catherine or Tyne Streets, having their headquarters at an ice cream shop at the end of Kensington Villas. Back row: R. Jackson, J. Connolly, J. Davison, T. Coxon, T. Woods, A. Martin. Centre row: J. Rawlings, J. Ashurst, A. Ashurst. Front row: R. Graham, A. Graham, T. Craggs, R. Davison, J. Bennett.

The Villa A.F.C. The team members are: K. Lloyd, I. Fleming, J. Newcombe, A. Swan, W. Frame, W. Henderson, G. Pears, J. Newcombe, N. Small, W. Race, H. Cooper, P. Casey, J. Bond, P. Traynor, T. Carlin, J. Casey, H. Hunt, J. Foxcroft, and the mascot T. Bond.

Willington A.F.C., 1948-49, with their trophies won during the season. Some of these players went on to play at Wembley in the Amateur Cup Final of 1950.

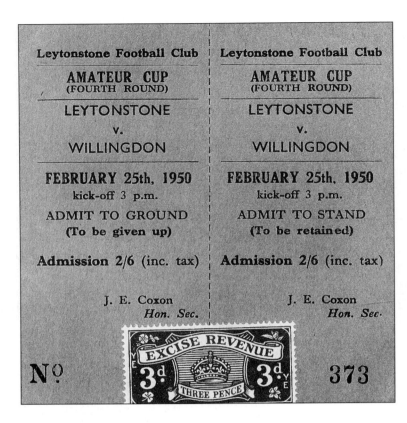

Leytonstone Football Club

AMATEUR CUP
(FOURTH ROUND)

LEYTONSTONE
v.
WILLINGDON

FEBRUARY 25th, 1950
kick-off 3 p.m.

ADMIT TO GROUND
(To be given up)

Admission 2/6 (inc. tax)

J. E. Coxon
Hon. Sec.

Nº

EXCISE REVENUE
3d
3d
THREE PENCE

Leytonstone Football Club

AMATEUR CUP
(FOURTH ROUND)

LEYTONSTONE
v.
WILLINGDON

FEBRUARY 25th, 1950
kick-off 3 p.m.

ADMIT TO STAND
(To be retained)

Admission 2/6 (inc. tax)

J. E. Coxon
Hon. Sec.

373

An unused entry ticket to one of the qualifying matches on the road to Wembley. Maybe Leytonstone would have won if they had spelt the name correctly, whereas they lost 2-3!

The supporters waiting to board one of Bond's buses to travel to an away match.

Wembley Final, 25 April 1950. The proud owners of the Amateur Challenge Cup, at last getting their revenge over Bishop Auckland who had defeated them in the Cup Final of 1939, played at Roker Park. The score at Wembley was 4-0. The goal scorers were Taylor, Rutherford, Larmouth and Armstrong. The first three goals were scored within thirty minutes and the fourth coming just fourteen minutes before the final whistle.

The Amateur Challenge Cup Winners:
J. Snowdon, W. Craggs, S. Howe,
J. Lewthwade, E. Yeardley, J. Dodd,
R. Alderson, J. Robinson, E. Taylor,
W. Larmouth, M. Armstrong, S. Rutherford,
R. Biggs, J. Hateley (President), J. Nicholson
(Chairman), G. Smailes (Secretary).

The programme for the 1950 Final.

Seven
Colliery

Mr P. J. Traynor hewing in Cross Cut East seam. This seam at Brancepeth Colliery was only between twelve and fifteen inches in height. For readers' information and those not familiar with the area, Brancepeth Colliery was located in Willington and Willington Colliery was in Sunnybrow.

A coal delivery, *c.* 1960. This was in the days before coal was delivered in sacks. For most colliery workers part of their contract was the delivery of a free load of coals every few weeks. These were tipped on people's doorsteps and had to be shovelled into a coal house. This gentleman, Laurie Wood, was from the south and it was his first encounter with a load of coals. I don't know whether this had any bearing on his emigration to Australia just a few months later, but maybe!

The colliery at nearby Oakenshaw which was part of the Straker and Love partnership.

In 1936 two minutes silence was observed to respect the death of King George V.

A pit pony and its handler.

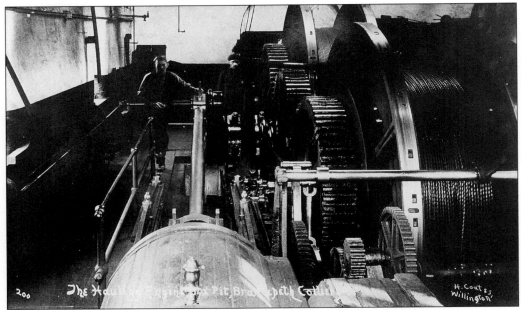

The Hauling Engine. When the tubs of coal were filled the 'putter', usually a young boy, pushed them out on to a landing where they were hauled to the surface by means of an engine like this. From here the tubs went out on to the screens.

The screens. Once out of the pit the coals were tipped on to the screens where the stone would be picked out and the coal sorted into different grades, the best of which being destined for bosses and officials.

The team of men responsible for pushing the first of the new patent coke ovens in 1910. That year there were sixty ovens, but by 1913 this number had doubled.

The colliery engine. One of the small engines used within the colliery yard and usually referred to as 'tankies', but the name of this one is 'Stagshaw'.

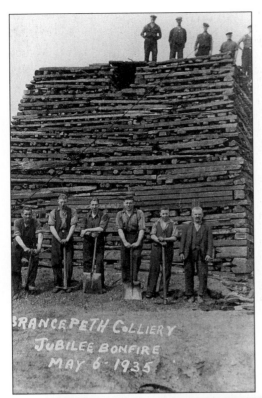

The Bonfire, 1935. Whenever there were any celebrations it was traditional for a bonfire to be lit, usually on top of the pit heap, making it visible for miles. This one was to celebrate the Jubilee of King George V and Queen Mary.

I am told that this is the opening of the Pit Head Baths. Up until this time men had to take their 'pit muck' home. Not many people had bathrooms so it was usual for men to bathe in front of the fire in a long tin bath with water heated by whatever means possible. The first baths were opened in the 1920s but these in the photograph came much later.

Colliery workers outside the blacksmith's shop. They are: R. Emmerson, J. Race, F. Nicholson, T. Todd, A. Husband, T. Golightly, R. Welsh, J. Clement and L. Clement.

Again outside the blacksmith's shop with, F. Nicholson, R. Hopper, R. Turnbull, L. Clement, W. Ludlow, A. Robinson and W. Cowan.

One of the Willington Colliery Banners depicting Conishead Priory where colliery workers could go to recuperate after an accident or illness.

Brancepeth Colliery Banner showing Burnhope Reservoir.

Setting off for the Big Meeting, held annually in Durham City. This was the highlight of the miners' year when Durham County colliery workers and their families, followed their banners on to the race course for a fun day out.

Waiting to board the train on Gala Day. This particular banner is draped in black silk denoting that there had been at least one fatality at the colliery during that year.

Preparations under way to demolish one of the big chimneys at the colliery.

Some of the men working on the levelling of the pit heap.

This building was erected for the people living in the Aged Miners' Homes, to be used as a reading room and meeting place. The site for these homes was donated by the Hamilton Russells of Brancepeth Castle. The first twelve houses were built in 1913 and the second phase of nine homes, together with this building, in 1925. It was 1939 before the last six were built. All the homes are still standing but the reading room was razed to the ground when it fell into disrepair.

𝕾𝖆𝖈𝖗𝖊𝖉 𝖙𝖔 𝖙𝖍𝖊 𝕸𝖊𝖒𝖔𝖗𝖞 𝖔𝖋

THE UNFORTUNATE MEN,

Who Lost their Lives in the Terrible

COLLIERY DISASTER, AT BRANCEPETH PIT,

APRIL 14th, 1896.

John Dowson	Henry Hodgson	Charles Linton	Tristram Spence
Thos. Nicholson	William Cooke	John Wearmouth	Thomas Carling
John Forster	George Lawther	John Jefferson	Michael Turner
John Rogerson	William Laws	Robert Ransome	Joseph Brigham
Ralph Lawson	Thomas Lawson	Wm Rawlings	

At approximately 10.00 p.m. on Monday 13 April 1896 an explosion occurred in Brancepeth A Pit, resulting in the loss of twenty men. At that time in the evening there were fewer men working underground. Had it happened during the day the loss of life would have been considerably more. These cards were sold in aid of the relief fund set up for the benefit of widows and orphans. A scroll commemorating these men was erected in the Miners' Welfare Hall, but we have no memorial to the many more men whose lives were sacrificed in the mining of coal. I have no way of naming these men, but I would like to take this opportunity to pay a special tribute to every one of them.

Acknowledgements

My grateful thanks must first and foremost go to my immediate family for their support and encouragement. Without the use of Kenneth and Pamela's collection of pictures, it would not have been possible to produce this book. As a member of the older generation, the help of Nigel and Joanne in this modern world of technology and word processors has proved invaluable.

Secondly to local photographers, the late Messers Coates, Foster and Toyn, who had the foresight to record on camera, the day to day events of Willington and its people.

Also to everyone I've had the privilege to listen to over the past years as they shared their memories and recollections of a bygone age with me, amongst them being: E. Aspinall, S. Aspinall, D. Brown, R. Caile, K. Cummings, J. Davison, B. Dunleavy, T. Failes, R. Lee, E. Lines, A. Morton, J. Simpson and E. Traynor.

And a final tribute to the late Kevin Bell, who took such an interest in his village.

While I have endeavoured to be accurate with names and dates, memories do play tricks, so if for any reason I have failed in this I extend my apologies.